CHORAL E

MW00414349

Praises

*Three
Decades of
Inspirational
Song*

27 STIRRING CLASSICS & EXCITING NEW STANDARDS

ARRANGED BY
TOM FETTKE

Lillenas PUBLISHING COMPANY

KANSAS CITY, MO 64141

C O N T E N T S

Song begins on page 4 in the Solo/Accompaniment Edition

High and Lifted Up

D. W.

DIANE WILKINSON
Arr. by Tom Fettke

1.
high and lift - ed up___ must Je - sus be.

2.
slight accel.
high and lift - ed up___ He took the blame.
Oo___

A little faster ♩ = ca. 66
15 Choir
mf
High and lift - ed up___ the lov - ing Sav - ior,___
mf

High and lift - ed up___ for all to see.___

19
Rec - on - cil - ing God___ and man for - ev - er,

CD 1:3

High and lift-ed up on Cal - va - ry.

Unison 25

Je - sus said, "I'll sure - ly come a - gain That wher-

ev - er I may be you will be near." So I'm

29

look - ing toward the heav - ens, up to the east - ern sky, Where

high and lift - ed up He shall ap - pear.

8

Praises

A. C.

ANDRAÉ CROUCH
Arr. by Tom Fettke

CD 1:6 2nd time

give to Je - sus, our King._____ King._____

27
Div.
He has giv-en us a new song,_____ A_____

song un - to our God;_____ A_____

35
song_____ of vic-to-ry, It's a song of praise, A

CD 1:7
song_____ that lifts up His ho - ly name._____

Hal - le - lu, Hal - le - lu -

jah! Hal - le - lu - jah!_____ Glo - ry,

glo - ry, Let the earth give Him glo - ry, Je - sus Christ,___ our

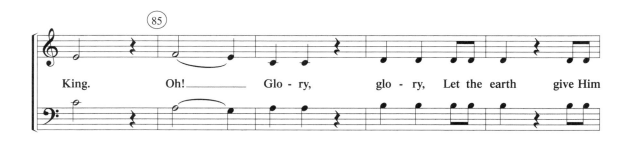

King. Oh!___ Glo - ry, glo - ry, Let the earth give Him

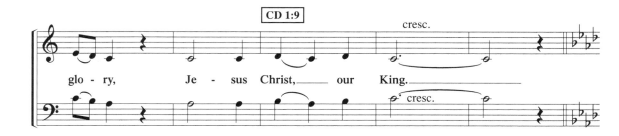

glo - ry, Je - sus Christ,___ our King.___

Song begins on page 16 in the Solo/Accompaniment Edition

I Stand Here Forgiven

G. N. and P. M.

GREG NELSON and PHIL MCHUGH
Arr. by Tom Fettke

depths of the sea. I have been washed in the stream of sal - va - tion, And

I am free. I must keep my spir - it filled with

all that God has spo - ken; Then I'm safe from

Sa - tan's lies– I'll know His pow'r is bro - ken.

cresc. free.
cresc.
cresc.

Song begins on page 21 in the Solo/Accompaniment Edition

Think About His Love

W. H.

WALT HARRAH
Arr. by Tom Fettke

With great warmth ♩ = ca. 54

CD 1:14 *mf*

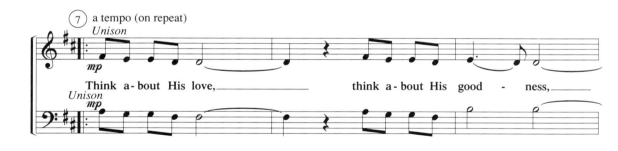

⑦ a tempo (on repeat)
Unison
mp

Think a-bout His love,_____ think a-bout His good - ness,_____

Unison
mp

⑪

Div.

Think a-bout His grace that's brought us

Div.

through._____ For as high as the heav-ens a-bove_____ So

great is the mea-sure of our Fa-ther's love.

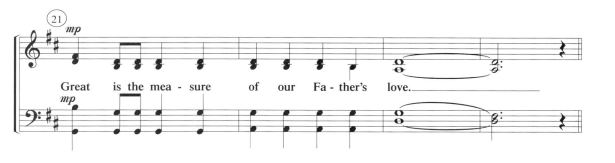

Great is the mea-sure of our Fa-ther's love._____

1. How could I_____ for-get_____ His love?_____
2. E - ven when_____ I've strayed_____ a - way,_____

Oo

20

through. For as high as the heav-ens a-bove So

great is the mea-sure of our Fa-ther's love.

Great is the mea-sure, great is the mea-sure,

great is the mea-sure,

great is the mea-sure, Great is the mea-sure of our Fa-ther's

great is the mea-sure,

love, His love.

Song begins on page 26 in the Solo/Accompaniment Edition

God So Loved the World

D. T. and M. T.

DICK and MELODIE TUNNEY
Arr. by Tom Fettke

26

Song begins on page 31 in the Solo/Accompaniment Edition

The Gates of Hell Shall Not Prevail

K. T., P. C., and C. C.

KIRK TALLEY,
PHIL and CAROLYN CROSS
Arr. by Tom Fettke

28

30

Home Where I Belong

P. T.

PAT TERRY
Arr. by Tom Fettke

32

33

Song begins on page 41 in the Solo/Accompaniment Edition

When Redeemed I Stand

G. D.

GERON DAVIS
Arr. by Tom Fettke

*Both 2nd verse solos may be sung by one person if desired.

Song begins on page 46 in the Solo/Accompaniment Edition

Building

C. C.

CAROL CYMBALA
Arr. by Tom Fettke

40

2nd time to Coda

42

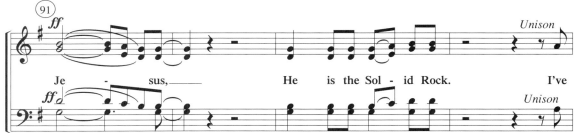

44

To Be Like Jesus

D. T. and M. T.

DICK and MELODIE TUNNEY
Arr. by Tom Fettke

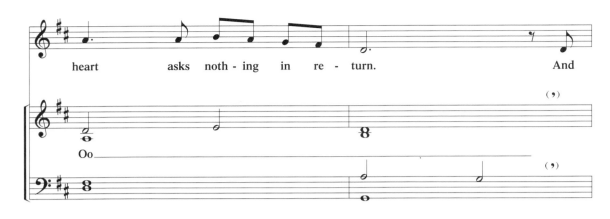

heart asks noth - ing in re - turn. And

Oo

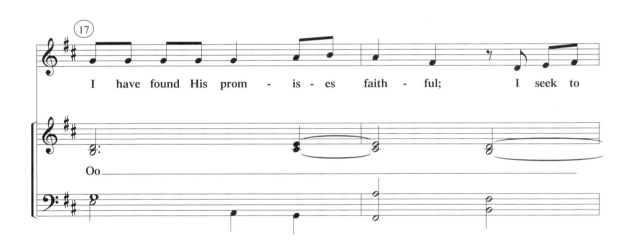

I have found His prom - is - es faith - ful; I seek to

Oo

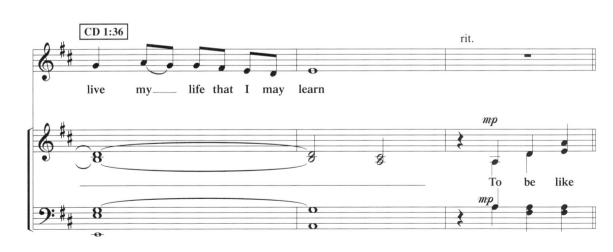

CD 1:36

live my___ life that I may learn

rit.

mp

To be like

mp

When I re-ceived His sal-va-tion, His heav'n-ly love filled my earth-ly soul; And I be-came a new cre-a-tion. My bro-ken-ness He made com-plete-ly whole. And thro' the dark-ness of this world I've been com-mis-sioned to be a light that shines for Him a-lone. Sur-round-ed by His in-fi-nite mer-cy, may my life al-ways be known To be like Je-sus, to be like Je-sus,

CD 1:38

To be the one I was cre - at - ed to be.

To be like Je - sus, to be like Je - sus;

My on - ly earth - ly goals ful - fill when I'm cen - tered in His

will. May all who see my life find Him in

me, in me.

Song begins on page 60 in the Solo/Accompaniment Edition

I'm Glad I Know Who Jesus Is

G. D.

GERON DAVIS
Arr. by Tom Fettke

never felt His peace with-in___ their souls. But I

want my life to show them___ how His love can set__ them free; He's the

on-ly one who can cleanse and make men whole. I'm

glad I know who Je-sus is! I'm

glad___ I know who Je-sus is!___ He's

53

54

Song begins on page 66 in the Solo/Accompaniment Edition

55

I Am

M. W. S. and L. W. H.

MICHAEL W. SMITH and
L. WAYNE HILLIARD
Arr. by Tom Fettke

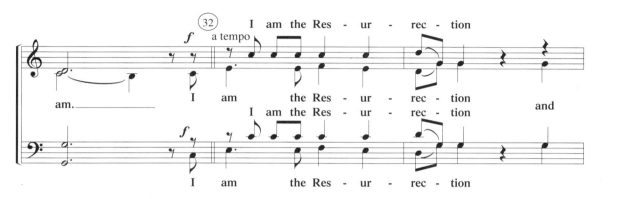

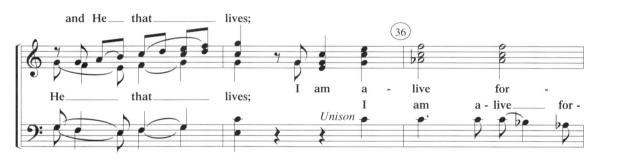

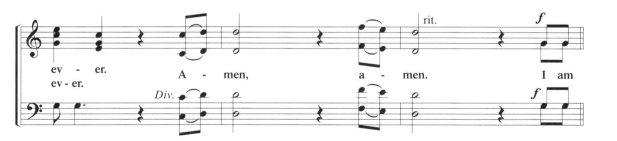

58

If Heaven Never Was Promised to Me

A. C.

ANDRAÉ CROUCH
Arr. by Tom Fettke

62

Song begins on page 76 in the Solo/Accompaniment Edition

There's Still Power in the Blood

K. T.

KIRK TALLEY
Arr. by Tom Fettke

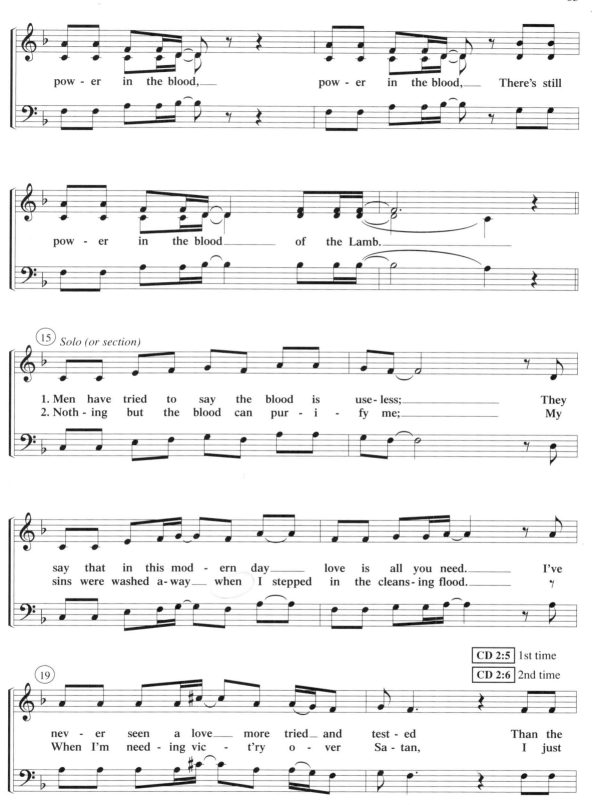

*"I Know a Fount" (Oliver Cooke)

CD 2:7

Unison

Unison

power in the blood, power in the blood, There's still power in the blood of the Lamb. Burdens are lifted, blind eyes made to see; There's a wonder-working pow'r in the blood of Calvary. There's still power in the blood of

Song begins on page 81 in the Solo/Accompaniment Edition

Joy of My Desire

J. R.

JENNIFER RANDOLPH
Arr. by Tom Fettke

Song begins on page 85 in the Solo/Accompaniment Edition

Heal Our Land

with "America, the Beautiful"

T. B. and R. B.

TOM and ROBIN BROOKS
Arr. by Tom Fettke

73

30
heal our land; hear us, O Lord, and heal our land. For -
CD 2:13
34
rit.
a tempo
D.S. al Coda
Solo mp
give our sin and heal our bro - ken land. Lord, we
CODA
cresc.
f
40
land. Lord, heal our land; Fa - ther,
44
heal our land. Hear our cry and turn our na - tion
48
back to You. Lord, heal our land; hear us, O Lord, and

76

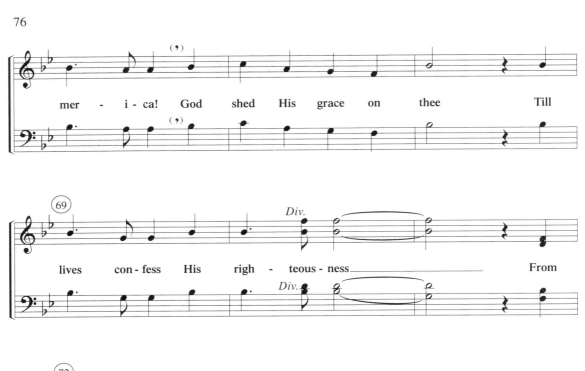

mer - i - ca! God shed His grace on thee Till

lives con - fess His righ - teous - ness_____ From

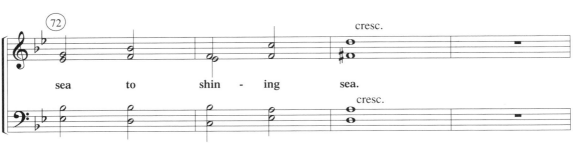

sea to shin - ing sea.

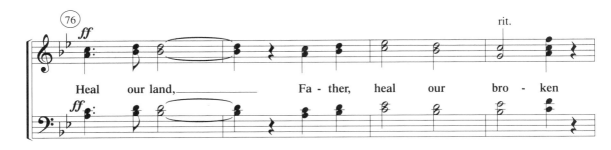

Heal our land,_____ Fa - ther, heal our bro - ken

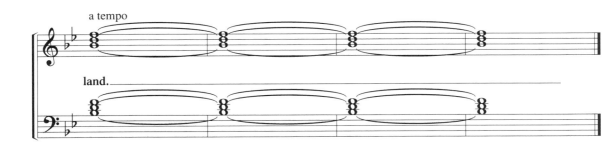

land._____

Jesus
(He Is the Son of God)

D. L.

DANNY LEE
Arr. by Tom Fettke

Soulful ♩ = ca. 60

CD 2:16 mf

1st verse:
solo (or section) mp

1. The bus - y streets___ and side - walks, they

2nd time: solo (or section)

foot - prints in the sand a - long___ the

sud - den-ly___ grew___ still As a Man came through the en -

Sea of Gal - i - lee, Where thou - sands came___ to

- trance of the cit - y,___ As He

hear His words and see Him.___ There He

coun - try._____ But the price He paid_____ and the

blood He shed is chang - ing lives_____ to - day, And with

joy and praise_____ you can hear these peo - ple say:_____

Je - sus, Je - sus, He is the Son_____ of God!

Je - sus, Je - sus, the pre - cious Son_____ of

God! _____ Sweet - est Rose ___ of Shar - on

came to set us free; _____ Je - sus,

Je - sus, He's ev - 'ry - thing to me. Yes, He's

all the world to me! _____ He's all the

world to me!

Song begins on page 97 in the Solo/Accompaniment Edition

Almighty God

G. N. and P. M.

GREG NELSON and PHILL MCHUGH
Arr. by Tom Fettke

*Original word was "Who"

*Original word was "Who"

84

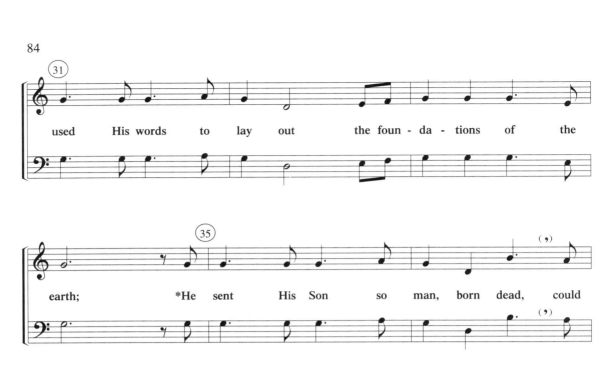

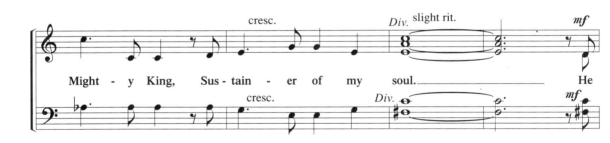

*Original word was "Who"

reigns in gold - en splen - dor, His heav - ens filled with wonder; He pur - chased my for - ev - er.

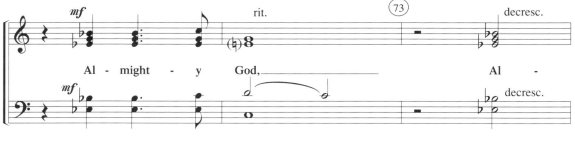

Al - might - y God, Al - might - y God, Al -

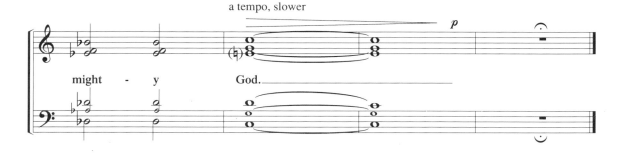

might - y God.

Song begins on page 102 in the Solo/Accompaniment Edition

Trust His Heart

E. C. and B. M.

EDDIE CARSWELL and BABBIE MASON
Arr. by Tom Fettke

88

Song begins on page 107 in the Solo/Accompaniment Edition

Where the Spirit of the Lord Is

S. R. A.

STEPHEN R. ADAMS
Arr. by Tom Fettke

care, God is pour-ing out His bless-ings on His

CD 2:27

rit. In rhythm ♩ = ca. 69 *Unison* ***mp***

chil-dren ev-'ry - where._____ Where the Spir - it of the

Unison ***mp***

Lord is, there is peace; Where the Spir - it of the

Lord is, there is love. There is com - fort in life's

dark - est *hour.__ There is light and life; there is help and pow-er in the

*two syllables

94

*two syllables

CD 2:29

54 *"Welcome, Welcome" (Norris/Reed)

Song begins on page 112 in the Solo/Accompaniment Edition

96

My Life Is in You, Lord

D. G.

DANIEL GARDNER
Arr. by Tom Fettke

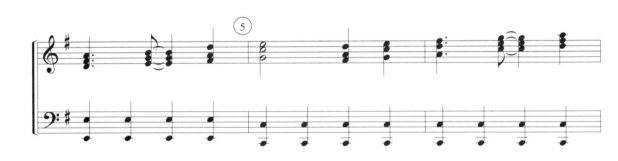

My life is in You, Lord;___ My

strength is in You, Lord;___ My hope is in

100

Song begins on page 117 in the Solo/Accompaniment Edition

Undivided

M. T.

MELODIE TUNNEY
Arr. by Tom Fettke

Song begins on page 122 in the Solo/Accompaniment Edition

Hallowed Be Thy Name

B. M. and R. L.

BABBIE MASON and ROBERT LAWSON
Arr. by Tom Fettke

107

*"fire" is two syllables

Song begins on page 128 in the Solo/Accompaniment Edition

Finally Home

D. W. and L. E. SINGER

DON WYRTZEN
Arr. by Tom Fettke

Just think of step-ping on shore and find-ing it heav - en! Of touch-ing a hand and find-ing it God's! Of breath-ing new air and find-ing it ce - les - tial! Of wak-ing up in glo - ry and find-ing it home!

2nd time to Coda

CD 2:47

Ladies unison

When sur -

Song begins on page 132 in the Solo/Accompaniment Edition

We Are Still the Church

K. T. and L. W.

KIRK TALLEY and LANNY WOLFE
Arr. by Tom Fettke

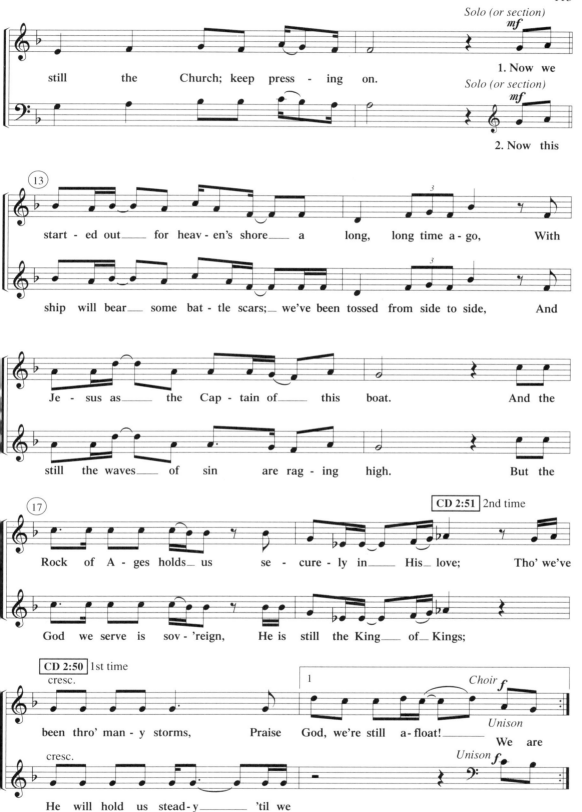

114